AR Quiz
BL  IL _MG_

Pts. _____

D1195514

Nature's Children

MICE

Susan Horner
and
Celia B. Lottridge

 Grolier

FACTS IN BRIEF

Classification of North American mice

Class: *Mammalia* (mammals)

Order: *Rodentia* (rodents)

Family: *Muridae* (rats, mice and voles); *Zapodidae* (Jumping Mice)

Genus: There are nine genera of mice, two of Jumping Mice and three of voles found in North America.

Species: 122 species of mice, Jumping Mice and voles are found in North America.

World distribution. The common house mouse originates in Europe and is still found there. Some native North American mice are also found in Central and South America, the rest are exclusive to North America.

Habitat. Varies with species.

Distinctive physical characteristics. Vary with species.

Habits and diet. Vary with species.

Published originally as
"Getting to Know . . . Nature's Children."

This series is approved and recommended by the Federation of Ontario Naturalists.

This library reinforced edition is available exclusively from:

Grolier Educational Corporation
Sherman Turnpike, Danbury, Connecticut 06816

Contents

Mice probably turn up in more stories, nursery rhymes, fables and cartoons than any other animal. But do all these make-believe mice tell us very much about real mice?

Think for a moment of Aesop's fable about the Town Mouse and the Country Mouse. The Town Mouse invites the Country Mouse to visit him, boasting of his splendid house and the exciting things to do—and eat—in the city. At first the Country Mouse is very impressed by everything, especially by all the fancy city food. But he soon learns that city life can be noisy and dangerous too. Before long the Country Mouse packs up and heads back to his own home where he lives simply but in peace.

Have you ever wondered just what sort of life the Country Mouse was going back to? What sort of house did it have? What did it eat? And was life in the country really less exciting—and less dangerous—than life in the city? Let's take a closer look at some "country mice" to find out.

Opposite page:

The long whiskers of the White-footed Mouse are very sensitive and enable it to feel objects in the dark.

Mice Everywhere

In the real world, as in story books, mice are everywhere.

Forest, field, mountain, brushland, hot or cold, wet or dry—nearly every kind of landscape and climate is home to one or more kinds of mice. There are mice that live in the far north and spend much of their lives in tunnels under the snow, and there are mice that spend their days in ground burrows avoiding the hot sun of their desert homes. There are mice that live in marshy places and are excellent swimmers, and mice that nest in trees and may spend their whole life without ever touching the ground.

The Northern Red-backed Vole lives in northern Canada and Alaska.

In North America alone there are hundreds of kinds of mice. Some live only in one tiny area. The Sitka Mouse, for instance, is found only on the smaller Queen Charlotte Islands off Canada's west coast. Other kinds of mice are found almost all across the continent.

If Aesop had been writing his story in North America, his Country Mouse would probably have been a Deer Mouse or a Meadow Vole.

Deer Mice are the most widespread of all North American mice. They live about as far north as the tree line and all the way south through Central Mexico. About the only place you will not find Deer Mice is in Florida or other swampy regions of the South. They prefer reasonably dry country.

Meadow Voles are almost as widespread as Deer Mice, but they are a little fussier about the kind of country they live in. They quite like fairly wet regions but avoid dense forests and dry grasslands.

Opposite page:

The Deer Mouse is sometimes called "wood mouse," since it often lives in the forest.

Mouse

Vole

A Mouse by Any Other Name

Mice are rodents. They are distant relatives of beavers, muskrats, porcupines, squirrels and chipmunks and cousins of lemmings and rats. The main thing all rodents have in common is very sharp front teeth that never stop growing.

The mouse's closest cousins are the voles. You have probably seen a vole, even though you may not have known it by its correct name. The most widespread vole of all, the Meadow Vole, is the little scampering creature often seen in barns, farmyards and fields. It is commonly called the field mouse.

It is not surprising that people mix up mice and voles; they are very much alike. So how can we tell who is who? Generally speaking, mice are more slender than voles, their faces are more pointed, their ears and eyes bigger and their tails longer.

The Meadow Vole is probably the most familiar rodent in North America.

How to Meet a Mouse

Walk through any field or woods and you probably pass very near any number of mice and voles without even knowing it. To actually meet a mouse, you must choose your time carefully. Most mice and voles are active mainly from dusk to dawn. Then you will have to be very patient and alert.

Patient because you will have to sit very still. Mice are timid creatures, ready to flee at any hint of danger. In most cases, their eyesight is not very good, but they have a keen sense of hearing. The slightest sound you might make—a sniff or a cracking twig or a rustle of leaves—will send them scurrying for cover. With strong legs to help it run fast and jump far, a frightened mouse will be gone before you can catch a glimpse of it.

Peek-a-boo!

Now You See It, Now You Don't

You must also be alert to get a good look at a mouse. Why? Mice come in a variety of shades and combinations of grays and browns. These colors blend in well with their surroundings and make them difficult to see.

Deer Mice get their name from their coloring, which resembles that of a deer—reddish brown with lighter underparts. But over time, even Deer Mice have developed variations. Those that live in shadowy woodlands are darker than those that live in the open.

You can tell by the color of this Deer Mouse's coat that its home is in the woods.

Small as a Mouse

We all know that mice are small. But there is small . . . and there is small. The tiniest full-grown North American mouse may be only 12 centimetres (5 inches) long, and about half of that is tail! A mouse that size may weigh as little as 11 grams (less than half an ounce). The largest mice are about twice that size.

Even within one kind of mouse there can be great variations. Deer Mice, for instance, come in a wide range of sizes. Once again, the largest is about twice as big as the smallest.

It's no mystery how the Red-backed Vole got its name.

Tails That Tell Tales

It is generally true that voles have shorter tails than true mice, but just as with overall size there is a great deal of variation. The Meadow Vole's tail is only about one-third the length of the rest of its body, while the Long-tailed Vole's tail is more than half as long as its body.

And there can be surprisingly big differences within one group. Some kinds of Deer Mice have tails that are only about half as long as their body, while others have tails that are longer than their body. The length of a Deer Mouse's tail can tell you something about how and where it lives. Those with longer tails usually do a lot of tree climbing. They use their longer tails for balance. Shorter-tailed Deer Mice usually live where there are few or no trees.

Tiny acrobat!

Mice in Motion

Scurry, scamper, scuttle . . . these are the words we associate with mice on the move. In fact, mice always seem to be in a hurry, dashing here and there and back again on their little, sharply clawed feet.

Many mice are also good climbers, and some are excellent swimmers. A few can even swim across streams. Some mice take to water mainly to escape predators, but others seem to dive in just for the fun of it.

And most mice can jump. In fact one family of mice can jump so well that they are called—what else—Jumping Mice. These mice have extra long hind feet, and the best jumpers among them can leap as far as three to four metres (yards). That is about 16 times the length of their body from their twitchy little nose to the tip of their long tail. Very few human long jumpers can come close to jumping even five times their own height.

Jumping Mouse paw prints

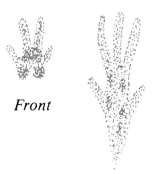

Front

Hind

White-footed Mouse paw prints

Front

Hind

Woodland Jumping Mouse.

Homebodies

Aesop's Country Mouse did not seem to mind traveling from his country home to the city. But most mice are not great travelers. Many spend their entire lives dashing to and fro in an area that is probably not much bigger than your back yard. The few kinds that do wander farther afield rarely go more than the length of a city block in any direction from their nest. The area a mouse regularly travels is known as its home range, and the mouse knows every nook, cranny, dip and bump in it.

While few mice ever leave their home range, they do not usually mind sharing it. When their babies are small—and in some cases even at other times—they are very defensive of the area right around their nest. But home ranges will usually overlap without anyone getting upset.

The Meadow Vole tends to be active both day and night, stopping every now and then to take short naps.

Mouse Trails

You would think that mice must have a hard time getting around in woods and fields. After all, their little legs may be very strong but they are also very short. The loose layer of fallen leaves and pine needles that usually covers the forest floor would be thigh-deep to most mice, and meadow grasses would loom as tall as giant oaks would to you—with a lot less space in between. So how do mice manage?

Have you ever noticed that if people use a shortcut across a lawn or through a field, the grass and plants soon stop growing there? Well, the same principle works for mice. They establish a network of tiny paths, sometimes even with bridges and tunnels, that go from their nests to various useful spots.

Some may be able to beat a path down just by their repeated comings and goings. Others bite off the grasses in their way and then trample down the stubs. And some do not bother doing all this hard work themselves. They simply use highways or burrows built by their relatives.

Opposite page:

A Deer Mouse out on a limb!

Danger Everywhere

Mouse highways are not just a lazy mouse's way of making life a little easier for itself. It is very important that mice move as quickly as possible and that they have a fast easy way to dash back to their nest.

Why? Because mice have a great many enemies. These include foxes, coyotes, weasels, skunks, raccoons, bears, shrews, squirrels, a number of snakes, turtles, fish and birds of prey. The list changes a bit with the kind of mouse and its habits. For example, mice that are active at night do not have to worry about hawks or eagles. And those that seldom or never take to water have no fishy predators. But it is safe to say that any animal that eats meat sees a mouse as an appetizing dinner.

This may seem unfair to mice, but you must remember that it is all part of the balance of nature. If all mice lived to grow up and have babies, there would soon be so many there would be no plants. The mice would eat them all. On the other hand, if there were not so many mice, many animals would starve.

Opposite page:

On the alert.

Mouse Menus

For creatures who never go very far, mice certainly do a great deal of running around. You can probably guess what they are doing: they are searching for food. Like many wild animals, mice spend most of their waking hours finding food and eating it.

In general mice are not fussy eaters. They will eat whatever is available, and they will eat a lot of it. This does not mean that different kinds of mice do not have their favorite foods. Deer Mice prefer seeds, but they will also nibble at buds and tender green leaves in the spring. Meadow Voles are mainly grass eaters, but they will make do with seeds, roots and even twig bark when grass runs out.

Almost all mice seem to enjoy an occasional tasty meat snack such as a caterpillar, cutworm or spider. And one mouse, the Northern Grasshopper Mouse, eats mainly insects. Although it will eat amost any kind of insect or insect egg, its very favorite is—you guessed it—grasshoppers.

Opposite page:

Some Mice will go to great lengths for a meal.

29

Clean and Tidy

Would it surprise you to hear that mice and cats have something in common? Actually, it is something they share with many animals— they like to keep clean.

A mouse sits up on its haunches to groom itself, using its tail for extra support. It washes its face with its forepaws, carefully rubbing its ears. Then it strokes down its back, and belly, combing the fur with its tiny claws. Finally it uses its teeth and tongue to groom its feet and tail.

Mice also like to live in clean homes, and many establish special toilet areas away from their nest. Many mice live in colonies and those that do often set up community toilets, sharing the work of building the runways that lead to them.

Some mice, such as Deer Mice, do not bother building toilets. They seem to find it easier to build a new nest when the old one gets too dirty.

Opposite page:

The long tail of the Meadow Jumping Mouse helps this champion jumper balance itself as it hops.

Mouse Houses

Adult mice usually each have their own home nest, at least for most of the year. This is true of mice that live in colonies too.

Mouse houses come in many sizes. Most are ball shaped and made of grasses and twigs and anything else that is handy: bits of bone, cloth, fur, string, paper—whatever odds and ends the builder happens to find. The inside is hollow and lined with softer material such as dandelions or thistle down, moss or cattails.

Mice build their nests almost anywhere that is protected enough for the owner to feel safe. Some mice hide their nests in underground burrows they dig themselves, while some borrow burrows abandoned by other animals. Other favorite hiding places are under logs and rocks, in tree hollows or stumps, in clumps of grass or weeds. Mice have even been known to take over deserted birds' nests.

This Deer Mouse has taken up residence in a hollow log.

This is how a Jumping Mouse hibernates. Its tail is curled up around its body.

Opposite page:

The House Mouse is not native to North America. Its ancestors came over on ships with the settlers.

Mice in Winter

Much like people, mice have various ways of coping with the cold and snow of winter.

Jumping Mice hibernate. They put on a layer of fat in the fall and go into a deep sleep until spring. The extra fat provides what little energy their body needs.

Most mice and voles, however, remain active all winter—though some more so than others. Many kinds of mice have stretchy cheek pouches in which they collect seeds. In the autumn they start gathering as many as they can and hide them in storage chambers near the nest. As long as their store lasts, they only have to make very short trips to their food caches.

These mice spend the rest of the time huddled up together in groups of 10 to 15 for warmth. Among White-footed Mice, there is a definite "pecking order" in the group. One mouse quickly establishes itself as top mouse and gets the warmest spot in the middle. The least aggressive members of the group end up on the colder edges.

Business as Usual

Most voles do not collect very much extra food in the fall. They are, therefore, almost as active during the winter as they are in summer.

Those that live mainly underground travel back and forth through their tunnels as usual. Meadow Voles and others tunnel through the snow to use the same surface runways they use in summer.

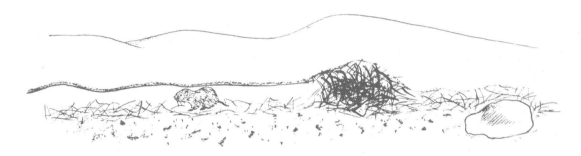

Mice use tunnels under the snow to get around during the winter.

All voles must eat their own weight in food each day to survive.

Squeal, Chatter, Cheep

You would not find it easy to eavesdrop on a mouse "conversation." Some mice hardly ever make sounds, and even the more talkative ones have very soft, small voices.

Those soft voices, however, can make a surprising variety of sounds. Most mice squeak and squeal, and many chirp and chatter as well. A few whistle in a way that sounds rather like an insect's hum. The Singing Vole is even named for its high-pitched, throbbing call. And, believe it or not, the Grasshopper Mouse sometimes sits on its haunches, throws back its head and howls like a miniature coyote!

Some mice have special sounds they make for certain occasions. For instance, many thump when alarmed— some with their front paws, others with their tail. And some female mice have a special squeak that lets males know they are ready to mate.

The Singing Vole—minstrel of the tundra!

Starting a Family

When mice are ready to mate—several times a year—the male and female share a nest for a few days. They will spend these days courting; they groom each other and chase each other around the area near the nest.

Depending on the kind of mouse, the male may leave after mating or he may stay nearby and help care for the babies after they are born. Either way, the mother prepares the nursery by herself. She either relines her nest with the softest material she can find or builds a brand new one.

These newborn Deer Mice are feeding on their mother's milk.

Big Families

The babies are born about three weeks after the parents mate. There are usually five to seven babies in a litter but sometimes many more. The number depends on the kind of mouse and often on the age of the mother and how well she has been eating.

Newborn mice are tiny—less than four centimetres (1.5 inches) long including their tails. That is shorter than most erasers! They are blind, deaf and have no hair except for tiny whiskers.

Fast-Growing Babies

Baby mice grow amazingly fast. For the first two days their mother does not leave the nest, and the babies nurse almost continually. Their skin is so transparent that you would actually be able to see the milk flowing into them.

A family of White-footed Mice.

Within four days, however, the babies have a little fur. In one week they have doubled their birth weight. In two weeks they can see and are moving around. They are still nursing but they can also eat berries and seeds.

Mice are careful mothers, especially Deer Mice. If the nest is disturbed a Deer Mouse mother will take her babies to a safer place. They stay with her by holding on tight to a nipple. If a baby should fall off, the mother will pick it up in her mouth by the scruff of the neck and carry it to the new nest.

If the father is still around, he helps keep the babies warm by cuddling up to them and helps keep them clean. He also repairs the nest and will go after any baby that strays and bring it home. Once the babies are old enough, he will take them on food-finding expeditions.

Out on his own!

Mice Forever

By the time they are a few weeks old, most mice are grown up and ready to fend for themselves. And by the time they are three or four months old, they are ready to start their own families. About the longest any can expect to live is about a year and a half. That may not seem like much, but it really is a lifetime to a mouse.

Few animals have learned to adapt to as many different conditions as mice, and few reproduce as rapidly. In spite of their short, hurried lives, you can be quite sure that next time you walk through a field or woods, somewhere very near some little mouse or vole is scampering about or snoozing in its nest.

So be sure you stop for a few minutes. Sit very still and watch carefully. And with a little bit of luck, your patience will be rewarded with a glimpse of the fascinating mini-world of mice.

Words to Know

Burrow A hole dug in the ground by an animal for use as a home.

Groom Brush and clean hair or fur.

Hibernate To go into a heavy sleep for the winter.

Home range The area that a mouse regularly travels.

Litter Young animals born together.

Mate To come together to produce young.

Nurse To drink the mother's milk.

Predator An animal that hunts other animals for food.

Prey An animal hunted by another animal for food. A bird that hunts animals for food is often called a bird of prey.

Rodent An animal with teeth that are specially good for gnawing.

INDEX

Cover Photo: Bill Ivy
Photo Credits: Robert C. Simpson (Valan Photos), pages 4, 23, 43; J.R. Page (Valan Photos), pages 7, 39; Bill Ivy, pages 8, 11, 12, 15, 35, 36, 44; Duane Sept (Valan Photos), page 16; Michel Quintin (Valan Photos), pages 19, 24, 31; François Morneau (Valan Photos), page 20; Albert Kuhnigk (Valan Photos), page 27; Francis Lepine (Valan Photos), page 28; Dennis Schmidt (Valan Photos), page 32; John Fowler (Valan Photos), page 40.

Printed and Bound in Italy by Lego SpA